The Bitcoin Guide

YOUR FIRST $20 IN CRYPTOCURRENCY

Gabe Fung-A-Wing

ISBN-13: 978-0-692-14925-6

Acknowledgments

M y Heavenly Father, my wife, my children, my parents, my brothers, and my tech, fit, and crypto crews. You all made this possible (especially my parents). Thanks for supporting me on yet another crazy project. I love you guys.

The Disclaimer:
Because I have to say it

*D*isclaimer: This book should not be taken as, and is not intended to provide, investment advice. Please conduct your own thorough research before investing in any cryptocurrency.

Table of Contents

Why did I write this guide?

You don't have to have all of the answers, you just have to know where to get them.

A few months ago, my Facebook feed seemed to be flooded with friends posting about Bitcoin and Ethereum. I kept scrolling past them at first, but then one of my clients shared his company's quarterly newsletter with me. It covered mostly commercial real estate, asset growth, and revenue updates, but the article ended with something that seemed out of place. A sort of, "Oh by the way" mentioning that commercial real estate investments are cool, but $100 in bitcoin in 2010 would be worth approximately $80,000,000 (33,333 bitcoin x $2,500). At the time writing, that number is closer to $240,000,000 ($7100 per bitcoin according to coinmarketcap.com).

Excuse me, *what*?

Seeing an established multi-billion-dollar company write that in a letter to their investors and employees made me sit up in my seat. I immediately went back to the articles I had seen on my friends' Facebook feeds and started digging. The first video I came across changed everything for me. Look up "Introduction to Bitcoin" by Andreas Antonopoulos on YouTube. All I had heard up to that point were passing comments about how Bitcoin was used by terrorist and thieves. (I later found out that they prefer US dollars or Euros). These reservations were not enough to stop my quest for understanding. In fact, upon further reading, I discovered that Bitcoin and other cryptocurrencies were actually being used, although on not nearly on the same scale as traditional fiat currencies, for everyday transactions like food, basketball game tickets, funerals, even Teslas.

This book was not written so that you can fully understand Bitcoin, blockchain, forks, ICO's, and all the misunderstandings that exist regarding the nascent technology. There are plenty of sources you can go to for that, I will even list several for you through-out this book. This also isn't another "How I made $7 billion in bitcoin in 3 seconds" story, either. God is selling the only available copy on Amazon for 22 million bitcoins.

If you're reading this, you bought the book because you are excited about this trend and you are looking for someone to help you simplify the process of getting involved. There is no shortage of information out there, but how do you know what's important now and what can wait? I wrote this book to help you *de-conflict* some of the information out there and find a navigable path. And, to save you the 80 hours of research it took me before I became comfortable enough to invest $20. My wife thought I was insane and she's a smart woman, I may be, but so are you if you fail to understand that this is the future.

Before I go any further, this is by no means the only way of understanding this world, this is just one man's perspective. It's my journey shared to help you see this opportunity and what it could mean for you and the future. My friends kept asking me how to get into Bitcoin and other cryptocurrencies and I found myself repeating the same thing over and over. Then I started writing mass emails. Then I figured others could benefit from this ground swell. Each time I explained it to people, I found myself getting better at it. So here we are, my best attempt to manifest my super power of simplifying complex things.

These currencies are designed with the stated objective of bringing the billions of people that are not currently participating in the global economy into the fold. So, like this crypto revolution, this message is meant for the masses. Don't miss it. By time you finish this book you should be comfortable purchasing your first $20 in bitcoin and then some.

Don't be an idiot!

Let's just get that out of the way.

Should I put my life savings into bitcoin?

If possible, I would jump through this book and smack you for asking that. No! Absolutely not. Take your time, if you are reading this book, you are probably still ahead of the curve. Putting all your eggs in the cryptocurrency basket is no different than putting all of your eggs in the Wall Street basket. If you are not sure how that went please see FY2008. As with most investments, don't ever put more in than you are willing to lose. Or as Andreas Antonopoulos put it when asked "What percentage of your wealth should be tied up in bitcoin?" His response was very well put, "A percentage that is equivalent to your understanding of how the technology works AND your ability to absorb the risk that it entails."

In a message to its new investors one cryptocurrency had this advice for users:

1. Store your assets under your control. Be your own bank. [ed. We will get into this part later]
2. Don't expect the crypto space to be fair. It is intense, volatile, and irrational most of the time.
3. Find reliable sources of information. Learn to avoid too much hype and doom. [ed. We will also get into this at a later point in this book]
4. Practice smart money management all the time.

More details on that article can be found by googling "Santiment resources."

Do I have to pay taxes?

I think some people just want to go to jail. Yes, yes you will have to pay taxes either immediately or eventually. Although most governments are unsure of how to handle, classify, track, and tax cryptocurrencies at this point in time, I can assure you that they will eventually figure it out. If you think that they are not working tirelessly to figure it out, then you don't understand the tenacity of governments in general when it comes to taxation.

I am all for limited government, but someone has to pay for your military and infrastructure. So, until world governments figure out a different way to fund the things we hire them to do, then the answer to this question remains a resounding yes. You should be prepared. Review the financial policies of the exchanges you use to transact. Talk to your accountant. If your accountant doesn't know, tell them to find out. If they don't find out, then hire a new one that does.

Anti-money laundering and counter terrorism financing

Most exchanges (places you buy and trade cryptocurrencies) will require you to sign some sort of anti-money laundering and counter terrorism financing agreement. If you are seeking to use cryptocurrencies for such purposes, I pray that the men with night vision goggles come and pay you a visit in your sleep. You are giving the rest of us a bad name. If you for some reason are still unsure if you are violating any of national/international laws, please consult with a treasury department official or intelligence officer. The world has enough awful, don't add to it.

Gabe's Tool Kit

What you need to buy your first $20 in bitcoin or other cryptocurrencies.

I have compiled a list of "must haves" in order to get started. This part of my journey was one of the toughest for me. I had no idea what I needed in order to securely get involved. The amount of information from informed and uninformed people could probably fill that big library in The Citadel from Game of Thrones.

Step 1: Bank account and or debit/credit card

Unless you already own bitcoin (BTC) or some other cryptocurrency, you will need a way to purchase them using some form of fiat (government issued) currency. I'm guessing if you've purchased this book the previous statement applies to you.

The most popular exchanges typically allow you to buy BTC using US Dollars, Euros, British Pounds, Chinese Yuan, South Korean Won, and Japanese Yen. These are just the most popular currencies, that's not to say that there aren't other fiat-to-BTC purchasing options. The exchange you can use will vary depending on the nation you live in. I will list some of the most commonly used exchanges in the subsequent sections.

And before the anti-government crypto maniacs jump all over me, I understand that there are ways to get into the game without having a bank account. For example, giving money to your friend and having them transfer the BTC to a wallet you own. Let's pretend that most of the people reading this book don't live in North Korea or Cuba; but if you do, know that there are other ways.

Step 2: Access to the Exchanges

Cryptocurrency exchanges simply allow you to buy, sell, and trade cryptocurrencies. I have broken exchanges into two categories for the sake of simplicity; those that allow you to convert fiat currency into cryptocurrency (main exchanges) and those that only trade in cryptocurrency (alt exchanges). In order to buy BTC you will more than likely only need access to "main" exchanges first. Bitcoin Foundation chairman, Brock Pierce, described these main exchanges as the, "on-ramps and off-ramps for the crypto world."

Most of these exchanges require you to go through a registration (signing up) and verification (usually needed to deposit large amounts of money) process. Be prepared to upload pictures of driver's licenses and passports. Registration is pretty quick and standard, verification can take days, in some instances, even weeks. Don't fret if it takes some exchanges a while, they are dealing with a lot of new volume and most are not prepared to handle it. Sometimes a simple email to their support address will speed up the process. This was one of the points of anxiety for me. I have over a decade of experience dealing with customer service in some capacity and the crypto world leaves much to be desired. Support for the most part is abysmal. I bring it up so that you understand that this is not an indication that something nefarious is going on, but rather signs of an industry that is going through that awkward phase babies go through. You know the one where they go from smiling to crossing their eyes, to poking that bottom lip out? It will get better. Just follow their instructions.

List of some exchanges:

Name	Country	Main/Alt	Trading Pairs (currency to currency options)
Coinbase	USA	main	5
GDAX	USA	main	12
Gemini	USA	main	3
Bittrex	USA	alt	269
Bitfinex	Hong Kong	main	144
Poloniex	USA	alt	96
HitBTC	Denmark	alt	314
CEX.io	UK	main	29
Kraken	USA	main	42
Bithumb	South Korea	main	14
Bitstamp	Luxembourg	main	11
Yobit	Russia	alt	1463
Binance	China	alt	237

For more details on the different types of exchanges google "Blockgeeks Best Cryptocurrency Exchanges: The Ultimate Guide"

To see a list of the top exchanges by 24-hour trading volume google "CryptoCoinCharts exchanges."

Step 3: Tools
Two-Factor Authentication

Almost all exchanges will recommend a two-factor authentication (2FA) app. All this means is that when you enter your username and password it will ask you enter a randomly generated numerical code from one of the apps on your phone. See examples of Authy and Google Authenticator below, both are available for download for Android and iOS. Setting up 2FA is usually done by going to your account settings and then to the security tab. Please do not use text message based 2FA, it is not secure.

GEMINI

Gemini token is:

82 825 17

Your token expires in

Authenticator

Coinbase
770 152

Coinbase
804 241

Bittrex
598 754

HitBTC
106 475

Poloniex
530 556

Bitfinex

Screenshot of Authy app   *Screenshot of Google Authenticator app*

IMPORTANT:

When you enable 2FA you will see a screen that will give you a QR code in most cases, with a "secret key" below that. You'll need that if, 1) You lose your phone and get a new one. 2) You upgrade your phone because it's been way too long, and you have to have the new one. 3) You phone gets stolen. 4) Your phone crashes and you have to do a factory reset.

Failure to write down, print, screen shot, take a photo of, or otherwise securely store your 2FA secret keys will cause great anxiety and stress. Because if scenarios 1 through 4 happen, you will not be able to log in to any of the exchanges you are registered with. Imagine losing your phone a day after you bought one bitcoin but before you had a chance to move it off of the exchange to a wallet you control. You should treat secret keys like you do your private keys and seeds for your wallets (more on that later.)

If scenarios 1 through 4 do happen and you have made a backup of your secret key, simply add a new account from within the app and enter the key manually or scan the QR code. Authy also gives you the added benefit of backing up all of your secret keys with a password.

Let's say you've already created an account, you have a functional 2FA setup, but what you read just freaked you out because you didn't write down, print, screen shot, take a photo of, or otherwise secure your secret key. What do you do? Well you have to generate a new secret key.

How do you do that? You log into your account with your username, password, and 2FA code. Once you are logged in, go to your security settings and disable your 2FA. You may have to do an email confirmation to turn it off. Once it's turned off you can re-enable 2FA and this time write down, print, screen shot, take a photo of, or otherwise securely store your 2FA secret key.

Screenshot of 2FA QR code from Poloniex

Silver lining:

If, for some reason, you didn't save your secret key you can always reach out to the respective exchanges and open a support ticket. I have researched that it can take any-where between 20 minutes to 7 days to get resolution. Please use this as a last resort, it's simply not worth the headache and stress.

Information and Currency Tracking

CoinMarketCap.com might be one of the most popular sites in the crypto commu-nity, and for good reason. It's easy to use and loaded with valuable information. It will give you real time price tracking of the top cryptocurrencies out there. But it goes much further, it gives links to the cryptocurrency's website, which exchanges it can be purchased on, volumes, etc. It's a must have in my opinion. It's available for Android, iOS, and web.

1274 Cryptocurrencies / 6498 Markets   Market Cap: $207,049,935,162 / 24h Vol: $7,014,238,166 / BTC Dominance: 58.1%

Cryptocurrency Market Capitalizations

Market Cap ▾	Trade Volume ▾	Trending ▾	Tools ▾		Search Currencies	

₿ Bitcoin (BTC) $7210.29 (-2.50%)   ⚡ Buy instantly with credit card
1.00 BTC (0.00%)

	Market Cap	Volume (24h)	Circulating Supply	Max Supply
S Website	$120,217,165,170	$3,238,290,000	16,673,000 BTC	21,000,000 BTC
S Website 2	16,673,000 BTC	450,043 BTC		

- S Website
- S Website 2
- Q Explorer
- Q Explorer 2
- ☰ Message Board
- ☰ Message Board 2
- ★ Rank 1

.ılı Charts   ⇄ Markets   Q Social   ✦ Tools   ▦ Historical Data

Bitcoin Charts   ≡

Zoom 1d 7d 1m 3m 1y **YTD** ALL   From Jan 1, 2017 To Nov 10, 2017

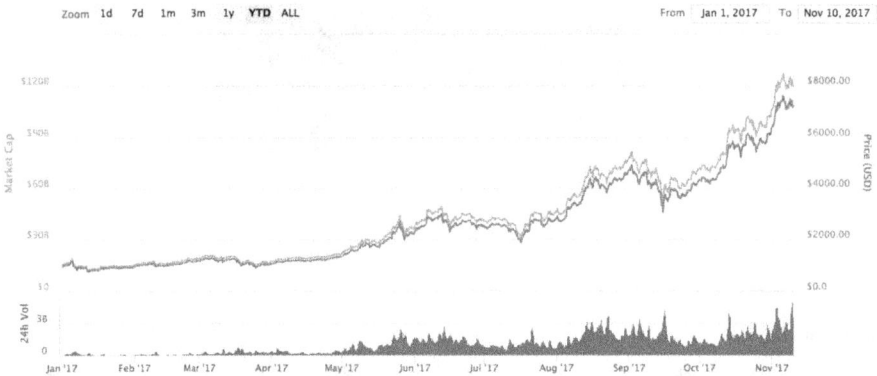

Screenshot of Bitcoin profile page on Coinmarketcap.com

Blockfolio (pictured below) is a mobile app that allows you to easily track how much of each cryptocurrency you are holding. Simple add a coin and how much of it you own and check it every 5 minutes. (You probably will. I do). It's easy to use interface is what makes this app one of my favorites.

Coin	Holdings	Price	Alert
BTC	$1,341.60 .07800000	$17,200.00 ↑ +2.39%	
ETH	$947.99 1.50	$631.99 ↑ +20.24%	
IOT	$2,497.54 571.00	$4.37 ↑ +5.31%	
DRGN	$618.60 1,413.78	$.43755386 ↓ -7.13%	
XRP	$681.35 1,741.46	$.39125133 ↑ +52.08%	
LTC	$349.52 1.09	$320.05 ↑ +30.82%	
ADA	$192.03 1,536.07	$.12501324 ↑ +10.57%	
SC	$171.92 15,127.00	$.01136484 ↑ +33.38%	

Total Portfolio Value: $7,919.16 24hr Change: +9.49% ↑

Screenshot of Blockfolio app

Your first $20 in Bitcoin

Slow is smooth, smooth is fast.

Once your accounts are setup using steps 1 through 3 from the previous section, you are ready to buy your first bitcoin. You may be asking, "Wait, do I have to spend $7,000 to get into this game?" If the title of this book didn't give it away already the answer is, "No!" Simply log in to a main exchange and go to the section that allows you to buy bitcoin, enter the amount you wish purchase, and that's it. You are in, welcome to the crypto world!

If the exchange you are using doesn't have a built-in converter like Coinbase, then just google "USD to BTC converter," and select your local currency. Although this may not be an issue for some of you, there can be some conversion sticker shock. I had to get used to thinking in $20 = 0.003233 BTC. Stick with it, though. Finally, note that if you are using a bank transfer it could take a few days for the purchase to be completed. Debit or credit card transactions are typically immediate.

You may be thinking, "So what's next?" Well, the BTC will show up in the BTC wallet in that exchange. From there you can leave it (I don't recommend this, I'll explain in a bit), move it, trade it, sell it, or cash out.

Moving BTC and Other Cryptocurrencies Around

This next section is where a lot of folks get sideways. Be patient here, otherwise you are going to end up on Reddit talking about some, "Bitcoin is a scam and Bittrex stole my money!" Don't be that person because you failed to realize that with all of this freedom comes responsibility. Love, Gabe.

Leave it

You could always leave the BTC or any other cryptocurrency (coins) in the wallet on the exchange where you purchased them, but most in the community advise against this. Here is why, although the blockchain that cryptocurrencies reside on are safe from anything except an attack from a quantum computer (they don't exist yet), most exchanges have been hacked at some point. The infamous Mt. Gox BTC exchange "lost" approximately 850,000 ($5.5 billion) customer bitcoins. At the time of the hack they were processing up to 70% of the world's BTC. As recent as 2016 Bitfinex was hacked, "losing" 120,000 BTC.

If you don't control the private key (the code that gives you access to your bitcoin anywhere in the world) then you don't control your cryptocurrency. Leaving your BTC with an online exchange is the equivalent of leaving your money in your online bank account. If things go really pear-shaped in the country you live in your bank/government may stop you from withdrawing your money. If you had your money in cash, then they could not block your access to the money. Unless you are actively trading your cryptocurrencies, you should store them off of the exchanges as much as possible. There is currently no downside protection for this industry yet, so don't be lazy here. These exchanges don't do it on purpose; that would be business suicide. But hackers gon' hack and China will be communist, so don't make it easy for them.

Trade it

Bitcoin is like a gateway drug into the cryptocurrency world. It is the most popular trading pair by far. Meaning in order to buy most other cryptocurrencies you need to do so using BTC (See image below of a BTC to XRP trading pair). In most cases you will have to move BTC from your wallet in your main exchange to your BTC wallet in your alt exchange. I will say again, actively trading BTC or any other cryptocurrency should be the only reason you leave your money on online exchanges. This is a best practice until the exchanges start giving some guarantees. As of now, even they recommend this as a best practice. Once you have found the coin you wish to purchase, select the price point per unit, then select the quantity, and click buy. As long as you have enough money to cover the quantity desired plus the fee, your purchase will be complete, and you will own the new cryptocurrency.

TRADING

BUY RIPPLE

3E-8 BTC AVAILABLE

Units	Max	0.00101098	XRP
Bid	Price ▾	0.00002960	BTC
Type	Limit ▾	Time In Force	Good 'Til Cancelled ▾	‹ What is this?
Total	฿	0.00000003	BTC

+ Buy Ripple

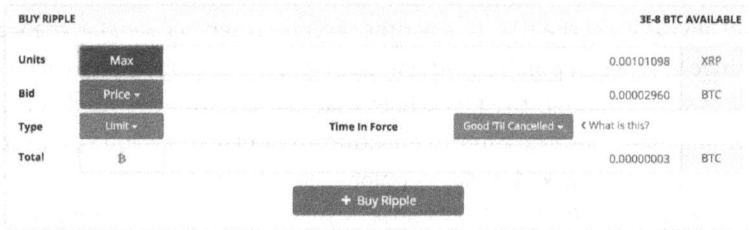

Screenshot of trading window on Bittrex

Move it

Moving cryptocurrencies around is very simple once you understand how it works. However, until you are comfortable doing it, you should live by this special operations adage, "slow is smooth, smooth is fast." They live by it, so they don't die. You should live by it so that you don't lose your money.

The process of moving currencies around is done by sending an amount of money from one like address to another like address. Each currency has its own address type specific to their blockchain (see samples below). Some reasons to move cryptocurrency would be to either store them in an off-exchange wallet (more on those in a later section) or to move them to another exchange that has coins that you want to trade.

Sample BTC address: 1QJacqMurJN6yPzXb4WiTGAYvU4rcWG7Y5
Sample ETH address: 0xf3b8D6E5C7b9b5FceE0B6cc4413B9883422B943d
Sample LTC address: LYJievThEFFPwiwusmEZgxgGsXMSpWzAN6
Sample XRP address: rPVMhWBsfF9iMXYj3aAzJVkPDTFNSyWdKy

Rule #1: Only move cryptocurrency from wallet to wallet of like kind
Meaning BTC address to BTC address, ETH to ETH, XRP to XRP, etc. If you jack this up your money is pretty much gone. In rare cases exchanges can help you get it back, but that is not guaranteed and will be a royal pain. We already talked about how bad the customer service is. Just go extra slow here. This is one of the most common mistakes newbies make, I wrote this book so that you don't do that.

BTC Wallet Address   ×

1Mh2LhwT1chCfzxMyRhGbSJQoLpsZQMhnP

Sample BTC wallet address from Coinbase

Rule #2: Test EVERYTHING

The first time you are moving money a new address I would recommend sending a small amount first to make sure you did everything right. It's better to lose $2 than $200. This also happens a lot. Don't be that person that sent BTC to your mom's home address because that's not how you internet.

Rule #3: Be wary of fees

Most blockchain networks and exchanges charge a fee to move currencies around. Exchanges do it because that's how they make money and blockchain networks do it because that's how they compensate their miners for verifying the authenticity of your transaction. So just be cognizant of this. Just because moving crypto currencies around the globe is cheaper and more efficient than the traditional banking method that does not mean it's always free. It costs to make money move.

Rule #4: Special instructions

Some currencies have different instructions for moving money around. For example: Bitshares requires a username, not an address like the examples listed previously. The best advice here is to go to the respective cryptocurrency's website and follow their instructions carefully. If it is the first time you are transferring a currency, follow rule #2 and you will be fine.

Once you have entered all of your information correctly and have sent your cryptos, have some patience. Some cryptocurrencies take longer than others go transfer from one location to the next. We are still talking minutes, not days. Some Ripple has taken a few seconds, Bitcoin has taken up to 30 minutes in my experience. The wait gave me anxiety at first, so I wanted to let you know that as long as you follow rules 1-4 you should be good to go.

Sell it

The two largest and most popular cryptocurrencies are Bitcoin and Ethereum, their combined market cap ($167B at the time of writing), is larger than the next 98 cryptocurrencies combined ($70B). Because of this, most other cryptocurrencies are either bought using these two currencies or are sold in exchange for them. For example, if you want to sell Golem (GNT) you would sell it in exchange for Bitcoin or Ethereum (ETH). To sell, select that trading pair in the exchange you are using, select the quantity of units to sell, the price you want to sell them at, and select sell.

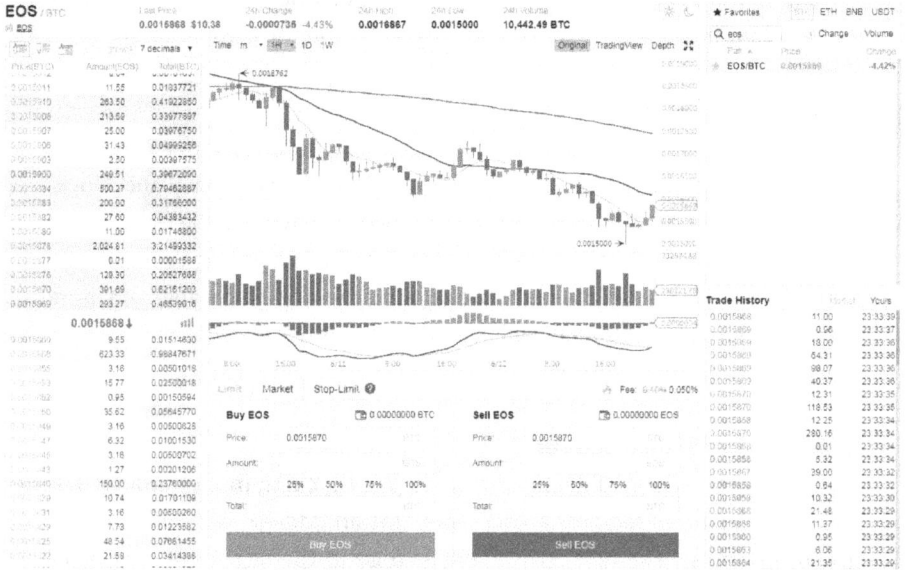

Image of Ledger Nano S hardware wallet

Cashing out

The best way I understood the cashing out process was by understanding the entire life cycle described previously. Walk with me.

Alt Exchange Process:

USD (or other fiat) used to buy BTC on a Main Exchange > BTC Transferred to Alt Exchange > BTC used to buy other alt coins. When you are ready to cash out you simply reverse the process like this: Sell Alt coins for BTC on the Alt Exchange > Transfer BTC from Alt Exchange to Main Exchange > Sell BTC for USD (or local fiat currency) > transfer to bank account. This entire process doesn't take very long (10 minutes) except for the parts on the front and the back end of dealing with the traditional banking systems. Purchases using routing numbers could take 5 days.

Main Exchange Process:

USD (or other fiat) used to buy BTC on a Main Exchange > When you are ready to cash out you simply reverse the process like this: Sell BTC for USD (or local fiat currency) > transfer to bank account. This entire process doesn't take very long (10 minutes) except for the parts on the front and the back end of dealing with the traditional banking systems. Purchases using routing numbers could take 5 days.

Which coins should I buy?

Learning to make informed decisions.

et me stop you right there. That is not a good question. It's your money. You probably shouldn't randomly throw it around. I will make suggestions but more importantly my desire is that you properly learn how to think about the different types of tokens or crypto assets you will be investing in.

In a podcast with Tai Lopez, Brock Pierce was asked this same question and to which he repeatedly replied, "Don't invest in anything you don't understand."

So, what follows are the questions I have learned to ask before I invest.

Who is leading the project? Do they win?

Research who the team is running a particular project you are interested in. In my opinion we are beyond the days of purely anonymous cryptocurrency creators. I can understand if no one wanted to be the first to step out of the shadows about a technology initially designed to usurp the central banking system. Can you blame them? But in this day and age there is no need for that. Find out who is involved, find out who their board of advisors is. This might be the most important determining factor when deciding where to invest your money. In most cases if the team is sketch or weak, the project will fail regardless of what problem they are trying to solve.

What is the use case (utility)?

This seems simple enough, but you'd be surprised how many people are really excited about investing in a cryptoassets they know nothing about. If you can't sum up what problem the crypto you just bought is solving in a sentence a fourth grader can understand then you should question your existence. JK but seriously though.

Which market segment is it in?

When I started researching this space, I quickly realized that not all of these cryptocurrencies are actually meant to be currencies in the way we think about them. In fact, most of them are cryptoassets that are the face of several hundred blockchain startups. For example, when you are buying Siacoin (SC), you are buying a token/investing in a company that wants to use blockchain technology for cloud-based storage (think Dropbox) ... or if you invest in Ripple (XRP), you are investing in a startup that seeks to use their asset, XRP, so that banks and governments can more quickly send money back and forth across the world. I recommend investing in market segments that interest you.

Here are some great articles by Techcrunch that really helped me categorize this industry in my brain.

"Mapping the blockchain project ecosystem" by Josh Nussbaum

"100 cryptocurrencies described in four words or less" by Nate Murray

What is the token/coin distribution model?

A lot of beginners have this thought process in their mind. "Bitcoin is too expensive, or there is Ripple, it's only $2.29, I'm just gonna buy 100 of those and wait for it to hit $20,000." Sir, ma'am, no! Let me explain why it doesn't work like that. Let me break down the Bitcoin token distribution model for you.

There will only ever be 21,000,000 bitcoins created, a certain amount of bitcoin is released every 10 minutes by miners (computers solving math problems). The amount that is released every 10 minutes gets cut in half every 4 years (it started at 50 BTC every 10 minutes, now we are at 12.5 BTC every 10 minutes), meaning the very last bitcoin will be released around the year 2140.

Ripple on the other hand has 100 billion coins, 38 billion of which are in circulation, and 55 billion that are held in escrow by Ripple. More detail on that google, "Ripple escrows 55 billion XRP"

The point of that comparison is so that you understand that the chances of a token with a max supply of 100 billion reaching the same price per coin as another token with a supply of only 21 million are slim. These details should help guide your investments.

Do they have a media footprint?

This is sort of in the same box as creators that still claim the need for complete anonymity. If you visit a super slick website, and trust me these are some of the nicest I have ever seen, but their news section is blank, pump the brakes. Secret projects that are claiming they are going to "SEAL Team 6 CIA Ghost Recon" Bitcoin and the rest of the crypto world, are probably full of it. They go in the same box as secret social media startups claiming that they are going to "KILL Facebook!" Although both of these may be true, I have a feeling we would see it coming.

If it's a hopping project it will be all over everywhere, crypto Twitter and Reddit will be buzzing, Wall Street will be bashing it, regardless of what avenue it's coming from, you will know about if you are paying attention.

Is the product live or under development?

This also seems obvious, but I'm learning not to be surprised by things in the crypto world. Whether a product is live or not is not good or bad either way, this is a very young revolution, and most products are not yet built. But knowing the difference could and should inform your investment allocation decisions.

For example, Bitcoin, XLM, and Ripple have current day application, their products are out, and are being used. Their increase or decrease in value could be determined by whether or not their assets are adopted. EOS and IOTA however, are currently being tested and their products will be deployed in the near future. Their increase or decrease in value may be determined by whether or not their products ever make it past the testing phase. In this fastest of environments, knowing where a product is on the roadmap should help you gauge the risk of your investment.

What are other crypto industry leaders saying about the project?

Don't overlook this part. The leaders in this industry have their ears to the ground, from Silicon Valley to Wall Street, Washington DC to Tokyo. A lot of them are crypto millionaires and/or do this full-time. Most of them still have big positive dreams and visions for what the crypto industry can mean for humanity. I think there is some safety in that. Oh, and they are the ones programming for, and leading, these crypto organizations. They probably know better than your nightly news anchor. Follow them and turn on the alerts!

Everyone is an expert. Kidding, that's not true, but in this booming business everyone will claim to be. That's why when writing this book, I wanted to be very cognizant about where my lane is. There are people that have been doing cryptography, digital currency, and computer science since long before even Bitcoin. If you plan on staying in this industry these are the people you want to learn from.

Some good articles on industry leaders

"Top Cryptocurrency People You Should Absolutely Follow on Twitter" by Bobby Ong

"30 Most Influential People in the Blockchain Space" by Antonio Madeira

"Top 100 Blockchain Insiders: From Marc Andreessen to Vitalik Buterin, These Are the Most Influential People in the Crypto Sphere" by Derin Cag

"CoinDesk's Top 10 Token Traders and Analysts of 2017" by Nolan Bauerle

Here are some of the people I personally follow on Twitter:

@aantonop @brockpierce @VentureCoinist @Crypto_Ed_ @CryptoOrca @crypto_rand @SatoshiLite @cburniske @CryptoCobain @whalepanda @iamSamsterdam @ErikVoorhees @CryptoMillion21 @gavinandresen @CharlieShrem @brucefenton

Emotions and the Top 20 coins (or those over $1 Billion market cap)

You have to learn to control your emotions in this crazy market. Every day there is a new startup launching the next "Bitcoin killer" and if you get in on their initial coin offering (ICO) you will surely be a billionaire next week. (And remember, we already talked about that sort of headline). Many people entering this space feel that they are late to the game and therefore don't want to miss the next wave. The FOMO (fear of missing out) is something serious in the crypto world and people running scams are well aware of this. They will play to these basic human instincts. When markets grow this fast they will *always* attract these kinds of characters. However, by paying attention and keeping a level head you can mitigate some of your risks.

Some of the crypto experts that I have been studying recommend that new users stay with the top 20 (by market cap) coins. These coins didn't get there by coming out of nowhere. Most have solid teams and a thought-out plan. They score high in all of the aforementioned categories. Check them out and be objective.

What's an ICO

The IPO for everyone.

nitial Coin Offerings, or ICOs as they're called, are a way by which blockchain startup companies can raise capital for their projects via the use of cryptocurrencies. In most cases the funds are raised using Bitcoin or Ethereum, although other currencies have been and can be used.

In 2017 there was a ton of hype around ICOs, and it's not hard to understand why if you have even a basic understanding of human nature. ICOs gave everyday people and investors from around the globe an opportunity to get involved in the early investment stages of a project. This type of access is typically reserved for accredited investors (people with $1+ million net worth.)

Three things happened as a result, 1) entrepreneurs raised more money through ICOs they ever have; $5.6 billion through 435 projects, 2) A lot of people made a lot of money investing in ICOs in 2017; the top performing ICO Ardor, for example, grew by 16,809% compared to bitcoins roughly 1,300%. 3) ICOs gave shady entrepreneurs the opportunity to capitalize on a sentiment loaded marketplace. Several ICOs are scams, where the entrepreneurs had no intentions of ever delivering a product, and they just ran off with investors' money. As previously stated, this is why it is paramount to do your homework before investing in anything, especially in the cryptocurrency world. If you thought buying regular currencies was risky, ICOs give the phrase, "high risk, high reward" a whole new meaning.

How ICOs typically work

Once you have done your homework and found a project that you want to invest in I recommend, above anything else, that you read their "token sale" instructions very, very, **very(!)** carefully. A misstep here and you will end up being one of those users broadcasting your failures all over Reddit. Don't be that person.

1. Do your homework (I might have said this already)
   a. Team?
   b. What problem?
   c. How will they solve it?
   d. What are industry leaders saying?
2. Read the specific token sale instructions
   a. Many ICOs require users to be whitelisted now, some don't.
   b. Make sure the country you live in allows you to participate in the ICO.
3. Addresses
   a. They will post an investing address that you can send crypto to. Please pay attention to the type of currency they are accepting.
   b. DO NOT SEND MONEY TO AN ADDRESS THAT DOES NOT COME FROM THE ICO's OFFICIAL SITE. People got ripped off by sending money to hackers via fake sites.
   c. Receiving address:
      i. ICOs will ask for a specific deposit address where they can send you your new tokens once they are issued.
      ii. DO NOT USE AN EXCHANGE DEPOSIT ADDRESS. If you do, you may not receive your new tokens. Again, this is plastered all over the ICOs website.
4. The Wait
   a. After you send your crypto there will be a waiting period before your new tokens are issued. This is typically done after the token sale period has ended.
   b. During the wait make sure you are subscribed to that ICOs email list, Twitter account, and Telegram if they have it. This is typically how they will send you updates.

Choosing the right ICO can be very profitable. Choosing the wrong one can be heart-breaking. The concept of being able to crowdfund a project from a global user base has undoubtedly changed the fundraising landscape forever. One no longer needs permission from the suits of Wall Street or Silicon Valley to fund a project, ICOs have decentralized this on a global scale. On the flip side, regular Janes and Joes now have the opportunity to get involved with projects at a very early stage. Typically, by the time regular people are allowed to invest in a company, it's been through several rounds of investments, and each time that happens, someone makes money. As discussed previously, the risk is much higher during the early stages of a project, but so is the reward and I am all about giving more people access to increase their position in life. I truly believe that that is a decision an individual should have the right to make.

For a more detailed explanation on how ICOs work google "Bits on blocks' A gentle introduction to Initial Coin Offerings."

For information on upcoming ICOs and their rankings go to:
CoinSchedule.com or ICOAlert.com

No Bitcoin did not get hacked

Secure your digital assets.

" The rewards of freedom are always sweet, but its demands are stern, for at its heart is the paradox that the greatest enemy of freedom is freedom." Os Guinness

Something you will often hear from crypto skeptics is that, "Bitcoin has been hacked." There has been no evidence of that, but there has been plenty of evidence that bitcoin and other cryptocurrencies has been stolen from online exchanges. You may be wondering what the difference is. Let me try to draw an example that may resonate. Stealing money from a cryptocurrency online exchange would be like a criminal stealing your money after obtaining your online banking information. That wouldn't be that hard for the criminal, right? Stealing money from the actual Bitcoin network would be like trying to walk into the US Treasury, steal $1 billion, and walk out. The network uses a level of encryption and decentralization that could only be broken by a quantum computer, and those won't pose a threat for decades. Our traditional banking systems are almost the opposite of that. This is an extremely over simplified way to say, the Bitcoin network has not been hacked, but plenty of online exchanges have been.

For more detail on just how secure and strong the Bitcoin network is please check out:

"The Internet of Money Volume Two" by Andreas M. Antonopoulos

As the quote at the beginning of this chapter alludes to, a system trying to replace centralization with decentralization and control with autonomy, leaves us with far greater responsibility than most of us are used to. Bitcoin was created as a response to world governments and banks after the 2008 Financial Crisis. Something different, something peer-to-peer. That's all great, but that also means that we cannot rely on the protections that we are all used to, things like FDIC insurance. Although these digital assets are proving to be valuable, you are not yet protected under your nation's securities laws in most cases. These protections may be available in the future and maybe the recommendations I am about to make won't matter in 10 years. But for now, they could be the difference between you keeping or losing your money. Like I said before, hackers gonna hack. Be vigilant.

Before we get rolling here are some terms to learn:

Addresses/Public Keys

This is the digital location where your cryptocurrency is stored. Think of it like your account. This is the information you would need to send and receive crypto. This address/public key can be shared. No one can steal your funds if they have this information. Funds cannot be auto drafted from your account without your permission. In fact, crypto addresses are public, anonymous, and can be reviewed by anyone, that's how secure they are.

Each currency has its own specific address type. For example, bitcoin is stored in a Bitcoin wallet. Conversely, you can't store Litecoin in a bitcoin wallet. Always remember this. If you send Litecoin to a bitcoin wallet address, **that money is gone.**

Wallets

Crypto addresses and funds can be more easily managed by using what are called wallets. There are different kinds of wallets and they each serve a purpose. There will be resources and wallet providers listed throughout this chapter whose sites go into greater details.

Here is a list of different wallet types that can be used to store your crypto assets, sorted in order to least safe to most safe:

1. Leaving it in an online wallet on an exchange
2. Giving your ex-girlfriend/boyfriend your private key/seed

3. Web wallet
4. Desktop wallet
5. Mobile wallet
6. Cold storage (Ledger S/Trezor)
7. Paper wallet
8. Losing your private key/seed in the ocean (super safe, only God knows the private key now)

Personal responsibility for your coins goes in the inverse direction from the type of storage option you use, the safer the storage the more the responsibility lies on you.

Crypto Rule #37: Do not confuse the security of blockchain tech with the security of cryptocurrency exchanges. Ever. Exchanges are websites and hackers are gonna hack. 850,000 coins were stolen off of the Mt. Gox online exchange in 2014.

Private Key/Seed

Private keys, or seeds, as they are sometimes called, are phrases or strings of characters that are associated with addresses on a particular blockchain. Think of them and guard them like you would your online bank account password. Guard them like you would a social security number. These are the keys to the kingdom of crypto. "Whomever holds the private key, holds the crypto." Do not ever forget this fact and don't let anyone tell you otherwise. I am not trying to be extreme but in lieu of you being your own security it's important to emphasize the significance that private keys hold in our world. Here are a few reasons why private key security matters.

Nefarious Governments

When you store your crypto in an online exchange, they hold the private keys so theoretically they control your crypto. Which means, for example, that if the government in the country you live in wants to confiscate the assets of the exchange where your money is stored and ban crypto as a whole; your money could be gone. Let's say this same scenario happens, but your money is stored in a wallet where you control your private key. Upon leaving said nation you could access your funds by simply having access to your private key. Various wallets will have different ways to go about accessing your funds should something like this happen.

Theft

Think about the scenario I just described, now think about what could happen if a hacker got a hold of your private key because you left it on your PC. They simply follow the instructions for a wallet that can access the particular crypto associated with your private key, they transfer your funds to a wallet they control, and your money is gone. Just like that.

Lost Device

What if you drop your phone in the toilet or lose it. Or your ex throws your computer in the river because you left your socks on the floor for the 1000th time. If you have been following proper security measures, then you have no need to worry. When you get a new device and reinstall the wallet where your crypto was stored you will simply have to put in your private key or seed phrase and you will be able to access your funds. But let's say you ignored the instructions during setup and never stored/wrote down your private key or seed on something other than the device currently in your toilet or river. Well then, your crypto will just join the 4 million plus bitcoin lost forever at the bottom of the blockchain ocean.

Important Note:

I cannot stress this next point enough. Please make sure your loved ones have a way to access your funds in the event that something should happen to you. Alternatively, maybe you want all of your crypto holdings to go towards a cause should you leave this life.

A lesson on why you want to do this can be taken from a crypto enthusiast that recently passed away unexpectedly. With him he took roughly $1 billion worth of Ripple and other crypto to the grave because his wife and kids don't have the private keys. It's quite sad when you think about it.

So, unless and until wills become mainstream on the blockchain and get automatically executed when you die via a smart contract, I highly recommend having a plan for your crypto assets.

Wallet types

Hot Wallets Simply put, these wallets are connected or need to be connect to the internet.

Web Wallets These types of wallets are accessed by using a typical browser like Internet Explorer, Chrome, or Safari.

- Online Exchanges – These are the wallets where your various currencies are held by an exchange like Bittrex or Binance. These wallets are ultimately controlled by the exchange. The exchange holds the private keys for these wallets. If hackers can get past your login on these exchanges, they can easily steal your money. Again, only hold money here if you are actively trading the asset.
- Currency Specific – Companies like BitGo and Blockchain.Info have bitcoin specific web wallets than can be used, and although you have access to the private key you are still accessing your wallet using a web browser. Not as problematic if you are using a clean machine on a clean network. Several alt coins, like Nano, also offer their own web wallet.

Software Wallets These wallets require the installation of an application on either your phone, PC, or Mac. They offer a bit more control and safety since these applications may not constantly be exposed to the internet when you are not using them. These types of wallets also give you access to your private keys and a seed phrase in case you lose your device or need to reinstall the apps. Many also allow you to store multiple currencies. Again, the cleanliness and security on your device play a large part in the type of risks you are exposing yourself to. If your kids or your wife use the laptop and click on all sorts of banner ads, and therefore navigating a browsing session looks something like Brad Pitt dodging zombies in "World War Z," then please don't store or access your crypto on THAT machine.

- Desktop – Many, if not all currencies, like Siacoin and Bitcoin Gold have their own native desktop wallet you can install and use to store that currency. Just go to any crypto asset's website to download their native wallet. This may be an easy option if you only plan on keeping a few currencies. But if you plan on holding multiple currencies then Jaxx or Exodus wallets might be better options.

- Mobile – There are a host of quality mobile wallets to choose from. Again, some are focused on single currencies, while others focus on being able to store multiple crypto assets. Same rules apply, if you plan on holding just bitcoin then stick with something like Blockchain, GreenAddress, Bitpay, Arcbit, Bither, or Freewallet (they offer several currency specific wallets.) The best multi-currency wallets are Jaxx, Coinomi, or Mycelium. Some apps like Abra, allow you to not only store you BTC, they also allow you to hook up your bank account and purchase the asset within their app.

Multi-Sig Wallets These types of wallets require transactions to be signed aka approved by multiple parties. Kind of like a shared bank account that would require, for example, 2 signatures prior to allowing a withdrawal. Some of the recommended multi-sig wallets include Armory, Electrum, BitGo, and even Coinbase. These wallets are a little more complicated to use, so please do additional homework prior to using.

Cold Wallets Simply put, these wallets are not connected to the internet.

Hardware Wallets These types of wallets look like USB sticks and they provide a nice balance between security and ease of use. They only have access to the internet for the brief moments required to process a transaction. They can also be easily stored and transported. They are highly recommended for storing and keep large amounts of crypto and all provide the ability to back up the devices with a passphrase/seed so that if a device is lost your funds can still be recovered by simply buying another device and restoring it using the passphrase. The most popular and recommended of these are the Ledger Nano S, Trezor, and KeepKey. All of these can be purchased on Amazon.

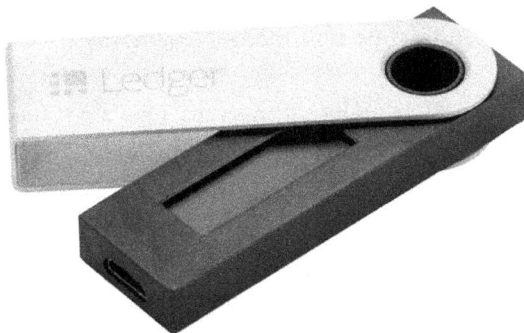

Adoption of Technology in US graph including Bitcoin

Paper Wallet These are wallets that are, well, made out of paper. Services like Bitaddress. org and Bitcoinpaperwallet.com allow you to create a randomly generate public and private keys that you can simply print and keep in a secure location. You may be thinking, "Why on earth would I do that?" Well this is as offline as it gets. This is as secure as it gets. As long as you are responsible with storing documents in general, this might be a good choice for storing large amounts of cryptocurrency for long periods of time. I have even heard of some crypto heavy hitters using this method in conjunction with a safe deposit boxes to safely store their massive fortunes. Two good places where you can have these wallets made are bitaddress.org and bitcoinpaperwallet.com

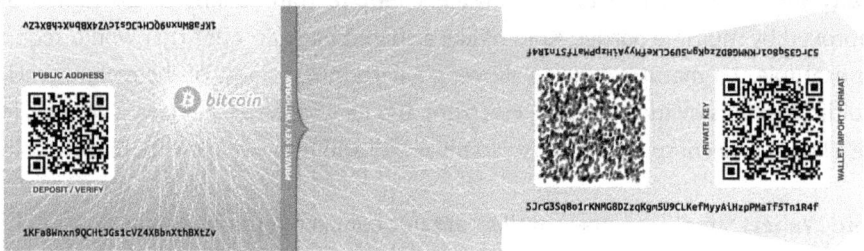

Image of BTC paper wallet from bitcoinpaperwallet.com

Offline/Online Wallets This method requires two computers, one online and one offline. The wallet on the offline machine is the only one that is allowed to sign off on transactions. Let's say you want to send money to Bob, first you would start the transaction with the online wallet. You would then save that transaction (like a transaction ID) on a hard drive. Then you would plug that hard drive into the offline machine, that you control, in order to sign (verify) that transaction. Then you would take that same hard drive with the signed transaction back to the online machine in order to complete the process and get Bob his money. Again, Armory can be used for this method.

Now that I have made you rightfully nervous, here are some pros and cons for keeping your money on or off of exchanges.

Keeping money ON exchange

Pros: If you want to quickly move in and out of positions or plan on actively trading crypto, then you can leave it on the exchange. If you plan on holding your crypto long term, then DO NOT leave it on an exchange.

Also, if the exchanges you are using support an upcoming fork you will get new coins immediately, and you don't have to do anything. Once you have them you can keep them or trade them.

Cons: Exchanges get hacked. Exposure to an online environment should be as limited as possible. The bigger the exchange the more attractive it becomes to hackers. Again, when Mt. Gox was hacked 850,000 bitcoins were stolen from online accounts. That is not a typo.

Also, if the exchange holding your coins does not support an upcoming fork and your coins are there during the split, then you do not get the new free coins whenever that new currency airdrops them. For an example of this scenario, Google "Coinbase support for Bitcoin Gold." Or you have to wait until that exchange decides to support the new coin. Google "Coinbase support for Bitcoin Cash" for another great example.

Keeping money OFF exchange

Pros: You are in control. You can decide to keep your bitcoin in one of several wallets from mobile/web wallets like Jaxx, to cold storage wallets like the Ledger Nano S. You have access to the private keys/ seeds to these wallets.

If you have your coins in a supported wallet during a fork, then you will have immediate access to your funds.

Cons: It can be difficult to quickly move in and out of positions because when prices are running in either direction exchanges, network traffic on blockchains and websites can become congested.

Silver lining:

Forks are free crypto. Blockchain startups issue new crypto during these new forks because they want to incentivize people to trade and use their asset. You can't lose, you can only NOT win, in my opinion.

The point of this section, and this entire book, is to give you a raw understand of the reality that is currently the cryptocurrency world. Don't be afraid, be informed.

I am not your professor

Learn to fish.

I t is very important that you develop a healthy habit of consuming information in this nascent space. I do not claim to be a cryptographer, developer, or applied mathematics PhD. I am just an enthusiast with a hunger for knowledge and a knack for being able to explain complicated things to everyday people.

There are some common questions that may have arisen during the reading of this book that you may want an answer to at a later time, good, that was part of my objective. You're not going to figure it all out now and that's okay, but I do recommend you find your answers eventually. If you are looking for a good resource to start with, Coindesk has a fantastic "Bitcoin/Blockchain 101" resource center you can find by googling "Coindesk blockchain 101."

There you will find more details regarding basic but important questions like, "What is bitcoin?" and "What is Blockchain?"

The Secrets are Still in Books
Here are some highly recommended books to consume:

- The Internet of Money Vol. 1 and Vol. 2 by Andreas M. Antonopoulos
- Cryptoassets: The Innovative Investor's Guide to Bitcoin and Beyond by Chris Burniske and Jack Tatar
- Digital Gold: Bitcoin and the Inside Story of the Misfits and Millionaires Trying to Reinvent Money by Nathaniel Popper
- The Age of Cryptocurrency: How Bitcoin and the Blockchain Are Challenging the Global Economic Order by Paul Vigna and Michael J. Casey
- The Blockchain Revolution by Don Tapscott and Alex Tapscott

The Herd

Watch the masses, do the opposite.

A t the time of this writing the total market cap for the entire cryptocurrency space is bouncing between $400 and $460 billion. From the time I started writing, I have seen the market move from $140 billion to its all-time high of $813 billion. I was surprised upon diving deeper into this space that it's not just comprised of bitcoin. I mean, yes, bitcoin is by far the single largest crypto asset, but realizing that 1600 other currencies/companies were all vying for their place was exciting. That level of competition and creation pushes innovation wherever it touches. Truth be told most of these start-ups will fail, but as with anything revolutionary, once the boundaries are pushed, things are never the same. 2017 saw a record year for crypto, the entire market grew by 3000%. Now, that type of growth will not always be there, but most people truly familiar with this space believe we are just getting started.

All that to say this: although the crypto space received a lot of press last year, "the herd" aka existing industry giants from Wall Street to Silicon Valley have barely begun experimenting with this industry. When they arrive, two things are bound to happen, 1) an influx and acceleration of funds entering the space, thereby pushing innovation further 2) mass adoption by the general, and mind you that means *global*, population.

What are some other use cases for Blockchain tech outside of finance?

To name a few: cyber security, insurance, healthcare, supply chain, and voting. You should check out Future Thinker's YouTube video called "19 Industries the Blockchain Will Disrupt" for a more comprehensive list of industries that will more than likely be changed by coming tide.

Are there any big companies involved?

Yes, and the list is growing every day. Check out the member lists on the websites of The Hyperledger Foundation, The Ethereum Enterprise Alliance, Blockchain Research Institute, and R3. One reason for this interest is that some of these giants are going to have to figure out how to securely manage the 20 billion IOT devices coming online by 2020. The current internet infrastructure cannot accommodate this in a safe and transparent way; blockchain technology can. The financial giants are also making moves, Goldman Sachs and Morgan Stanley are currently trying to figure out how to launch cryptocurrency trading desks. The volume that these two firms alone will bring to the market dwarfs the entire crypto market. Once they enter the fray, what do you think the rest of the world's banking giants will do?

What about the masses? We are not quite there yet for the masses, which is good news for those reading this book. If we could draw a comparison, the closest example of where we are with adoption would be the internet revolution in the early to mid-90s. Things to consider about the masses: with just about each passing revolutionary technology, the adoption curve is faster and more violent than the than the previous. It took decades for the masses to have access to the telephone. Now think about how long it took for the masses to have access to the internet.

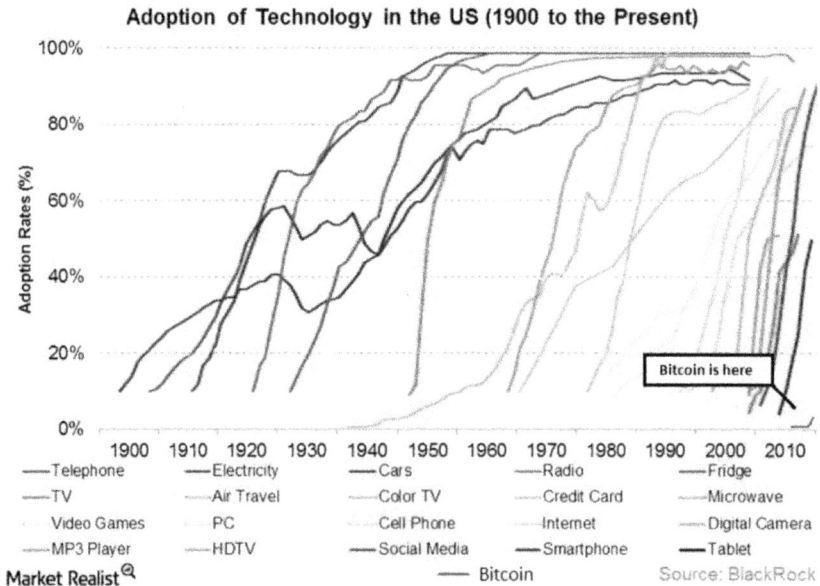

Adoption of Technology in US graph including Bitcoin

Know this: there are only 24.5 million unique Bitcoin wallet addresses according to Blockchain.info. Most people have more than one Bitcoin address (I have 5), and there are currently 2 to 3.5 billion people around the world that have access to the internet, but do not have easy access to basic banking. According to The Independent, 1/3 of British millennials will have holdings in cryptocurrency in 2018.

According to the 2017 Global Cryptocurrency Benchmarking Study by The University of Cambridge, most of the payment activity in the cryptocurrency world is occurring outside of The West.

Figure 68: Origin of customers segmented by payment activity types

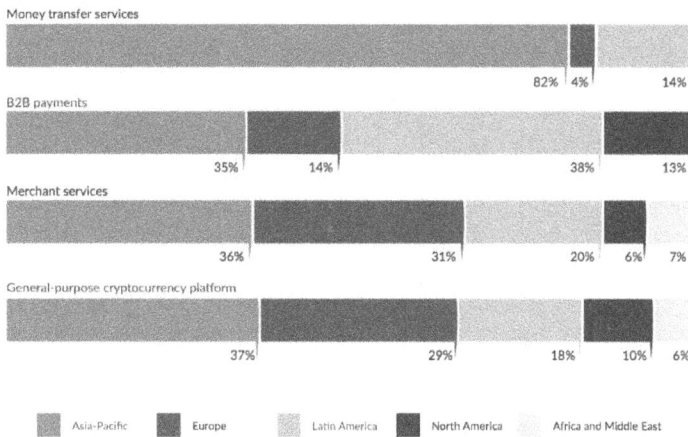

Graph from 2017 Global Cryptocurrency Benchmarking Study by The University of Cambridge showing global cryptopayment activity by region

The Herd is coming...

CONCLUSION (FOR NOW)

The world has now been opened to a new way of operating. Barriers for entering the investment space have never been lower; the unbanked will now be able to participate more easily in local, national, and global economies. The masses are calling for a level of transparency and security of information that wasn't possible before 2009. For those of us that live in The West, this revolution may not seem as obvious, but it is coming because change doesn't care about your feelings.

Experts often compare blockchain technology movement to the internet boom and bust of the late 90s and early 2000s, but they often leave out this important fact: this one is global and more significant. Think about who had access to the internet, PCs, and mobile devices when that boom happened. Basically, well off people in mostly Western nations. The blockchain wave can be adopted by anyone with access to the internet.

I hope that this book has accomplished its stated mission of helping you gain a quick and basic understanding of the cryptocurrency industry. I wrote this book because I knew how overwhelming trying to digest this entire industry can be. You don't have to know everything to be able to take advantage of this wave, and hopefully I have left you with a good starting point.

Due to the nature of this industry and the velocity of change within it, I will be creating updated editions as major processes and procedures change or are no longer relevant.

I will leave you with this:

1) Stay hungry for knowledge – It's your money and your future, be informed.
2) Test everything – We are pioneers, toes first, before you dive in.
3) Be quick, don't hurry – Monumental shifts like this only happen so often and they happen fast, take careful advantage.

Thank you for taking the time to appreciate this book, I pray it helped. If you want to show Gabe some additional love, scan below or leave a review. I can be reached on Twitter @gabefaw. Thank you.

BTC Address

A HOME FOR YOUR PRIVATE KEYS, SEEDS, AND ADDRESSES

Write your private keys here and store this book somewhere safe. If you have written your private keys here please do NOT share your copy of this book.

Crypto Asset

_____

Wallet Type/Location

_____

Private Key/Seed

_____

Crypto Asset

_____

Wallet Type/Location

_____

Private Key/Seed

_____

Crypto Asset

_____

Wallet Type/Location

_____

Private Key/Seed

_____

Crypto Asset

Wallet Type/Location

Private Key/Seed

Crypto Asset

Wallet Type/Location

Private Key/Seed

Crypto Asset

Wallet Type/Location

Private Key/Seed

Crypto Asset

Wallet Type/Location

Private Key/Seed

Crypto Asset

_____

Wallet Type/Location

_____

Private Key/Seed

_____

Crypto Asset

_____

Wallet Type/Location

_____

Private Key/Seed

_____

Crypto Asset

_____

Wallet Type/Location

_____

Private Key/Seed

_____

Crypto Asset

_____

Wallet Type/Location

_____

Private Key/Seed

_____

Crypto Asset

Wallet Type/Location

Private Key/Seed

Crypto Asset

Wallet Type/Location

Private Key/Seed

Crypto Asset

Wallet Type/Location

Private Key/Seed

Crypto Asset

Wallet Type/Location

Private Key/Seed

Crypto Asset

Wallet Type/Location

Private Key/Seed

www.ingramcontent.com/pod-product-compliance
Lightning Source LLC
Chambersburg PA
CBHW070948210326
41520CB00021B/7103